Before I Forget

Howard J. Kogan

Square Circle Press
Schenectady, New York

Before I Forget

Published by
Square Circle Press LLC
PO Box 913
Schenectady, New York 12301
www.SquareCirclePress.com

First paperback edition, 2023.
Printed in the United States of America on acid-free, durable paper.
ISBN-13: 978-0-9989670-3-5
ISBN-10: 0-9989670-3-3
Library of Congress Control Number: 2023933169

Publisher's Acknowledgments
Cover design by Richard Vang, Square Circle Press. Cover image photograph courtesy of Richard Vang.

"Mourning Becomes Her" was previously published in *Naugatuck River Review*. "Shoah" was previously published in *The American Jewish World*. "Say Grace" was previously published in *Misfit Magazine*. "Old Jack" was previously published in *General Store Poems* by Benevolent Bird Press.

The author's acknowledgments appear in the Preface.

This book is dedicated to my wife, Libby, who has been endlessly encouraging and supportive over our sixty years together. It is a debt I can never adequately repay. I cannot imagine my life without her and hope I never have to.

I have not always felt like a lucky man, but I am a lucky man. I have been blessed by my family, my friendships, and by the many poets and readers who have given me their presence and encouragement.

Table of Contents

Preface, vii

Canada Geese, 11
Terminal Diner, 12
Diplomacy, 14
Augury, 16
Visiting My Sister, 17
Slide Show, 18
Say Grace, 20
Her Name, 22
Red Rover, 25
Mourning Becomes Her, 26
Black Olives, 28
Slickrock, 29
The Girls, 30
Kitsilano, 32
Rattled, 34
New Year's Day, 35
At the Cancer Clinic, 36
Shoah, 38
Another Kind of Jewish Family, 40
One Autumn in New York, 41
Anticipation, 42
Flying in Winter, 43
Her Collection, 44
One Morning, 45
What Remains, 46

(Continued on next page)

(Contents, continued)

I Listened to a TED Talk on Dying So You Don't Have To, 48
Old Jack, 50
Sweet, 52
Pandemic, 53
Buoyancy, 54
Chasing Rabbits, 55
Ticket to Ride, 56
Deer Hunting, 58
Shadow, 64
On the Royal Road, 66
The Birthday Party, 70
Whiskey Down!, 72
An Eclipse in Stephentown, 74
The Boy Who Loved Pigeons, 75

About the Poet, 81

Preface

I have spent much of my life living in the future, but at age 82, the past is not only more present than the future, it's also a lot longer. Of course, the past is probably as much fantasy as the future. The present is a country I visit but rarely for long. The tug of the past seems to grow with each passing day.

There are so many people and experiences, real and imagined, who have contributed to my life and my writing that I could devote the entire book to that alone. For now, let me thank those who have read many of these poems and offered helpful and much needed revisions or suggestions. Every writer should be so lucky.

My wife, Libby, who is the first to hear most of my poems and who has generously supported my many and diverse interests over the long course of our relationship.

Trina Porte, a fine poet, editor and artist whose feedback and friendship over many years has been a gift. The title of this book is her idea.

Kathy Quinn, a colleague and friend for decades whose encouragement and interest has been sustaining, deep and enduring.

My main poetry group, which continues to meet bi-weekly and consists of Tim Verhagen, Tom Corrado, Barbara Vink and Tom Bonville, have read and offered feedback on many of the poems in this book.

The Wayland Library Poetry Group, led so ably by Joan Kimball, has similarly contributed to many of these poems. I also want to thank Eve Rifkah, a fine poet and teacher; Elliott Simons, a dear friend and poet; and Patricia Eng, a member of the Wayland Group, for their input.

Bernadette Mayer and Philip Good have remained strong influences on my writing though we no longer work together. Bernadette's recent death is a great loss for her family, her friends and poetry. As a person and a poet she was one of a kind.

There are others who have given me an opportunity to read my work at open mic nights and, in the process, to better grasp the oral heart of poetry: Dennis Sullivan, Mike Burke, Edie Abrams, Tom Corrado, Dan Wilcox, Nancy Klepsch, Paul Szlosek, Ron Whittle, John McCaffrey, Bob Sharkey, Roger Davis, Bob Whelan and others.

I have also been grateful for my long relationship with the editor and publisher Richard Vang of Square Circle Press. This is the third book we have done together over the last dozen years and, as in the previous two books, his influence and expertise are evident throughout. I am very grateful that we met all those years ago at a poetry event at Smitty's Tavern in Voorheesville, New York. He has become a dear friend along the way.

Finally, I am indebted to the many muses who, in a way that is often barely conscious (a face, a dream, a conversation), seem to ignite memories, thoughts or fantasies which may end in a poem or lie in wait in my unconscious to emerge at the most unexpected but helpful moments. Forgive me for not mentioning each of my muses by name, but I couldn't if I tried.

One thing is certain, one must have the time and inclination for what in our hectic era is called "down time," as though the machinery of the Self was broken. Mark Twain once quipped, "sometimes I sit and think and sometimes I just sit." Both are rare gifts and necessities for any writer, as is exposure to fellow poets and the long tradition of poetry, on whose shoulders we uneasily stand.

Howard J. Kogan
Ashland, Massachusetts (2023)

Before I Forget

Canada Geese

We lift our eyes to the Canada Geese drifting down
onto the field like tea leaves settling into a revelation,
then watch the high-flying enchanters transform
into waddling villagers squabbling over spilled corn.
Everything looks different up close,
like the classy, beautiful couple we envied
the moment we were seated near them,
the maître d' fawned, knew their names,
while we were out for an anniversary dinner
in a country club where we didn't belong.
They ordered elegantly, whispered intimately,
and we hated them, the way country clubs hate
Canada Geese, until their talk got loud and nasty
and we stopped talking to listen and gloat.
They sounded like the geese that walk
around crapping on the greens,
very different from the ones that fly overhead,
winged gurus dispensing melancholy answers
to questions we didn't ask.
When all we want to know is whether
dying is like falling asleep or waking.

Terminal Diner

The prompt is a sepia-toned postcard, a photograph of the Terminal Diner. It's an old-style Art Deco aluminum-paneled diner wedged against the gritty wall of an old large building with an auto mechanic's shop on street level and apartments above. A fire escape clings tenaciously to the building's front wall of the second and third floors, the frame of the postcard cuts off the building at that point so we don't see its full height. A laurel of coiled barbed wire on the diner's roof testifies to its feelings about the neighborhood. The sidewalk in front is patched and uneven, the few cars on the street are old but not classic. It's a cloudy day.

Let's add a driving rain to the gray day

to make the mood clear, to explain the few

men that quickly duck in this diner hoping

to meet no one.

Hesitant men who feel the need to order

as if this diner had been their destination,

as if they had always intended to sit at

this counter separated by a moat of empty stools.

The waitress is a skinny blond in her sixties

who keeps a cigarette lit in a corner ashtray

returning to it between customers as if it were

her daughter or her lover, the one that will kill her.

I stare at my black coffee as if it were something to be understood.

If the rain lasts much longer, I'll have to order something,

perhaps a slice of plastic lemon meringue pie that flashes

its glistening flank at me like an aging stripper.

But the storm takes pity on us, the rain ends,

the sky lightens and we leave this hospice of the heart

like afternoon movie-goers blinking in the surprising

brightness of an ordinary day.

Diplomacy

Li Bai (701-762), known as Li Bo or Li Po, was a Chinese poet who took traditional poetic forms to new heights. He and his friend Du Fu (712-770) were the two most prominent figures in the flourishing of Chinese poetry in the Tang dynasty.

Kubayashi Issa (1763–1828) was a Japanese poet and lay Buddhist priest known for his haiku poems and journals. He is better known by his pen name Issa (一茶), meaning Cup-of-tea. He is considered one of the four haiku masters of Japan. One of his better-known haikus is:

> *Goes out,*
> *comes back—*
> *the love life of a cat.*

Kubayashi and I have been trying to get Li Bai to have dinner,

he's willing but the time or the day is never right.

I thought we could tempt him with Italian,

it's not what he usually eats,

but Du Fu gets reflux from Italian,

and Li never goes anywhere without Du.

I hoped the dinner would lift Kubayashi's mood,

between his wife and the fire, he's had a rough year.

Of course, he always wants Sushi, but for Li Bai,

older and venerated, he's willing to make an exception.

We decide to see if Li would prefer Chinese, he's used to it

and if we go Cantonese, Du Fu should be okay.

Yet the note that replied to our latest invitation is from Du.

Du is not the problem, the problem is that Li has recently heard

of French fries, wants to try them, but he's too polite to ask.

Kubayashi and I are amused by this, but if Li and Du, at their age,

are willing to clog their arteries, that's okay with us.

Frankly, I'm not sure Kubayashi knows what French fries are,

since he asks me to suggest a French restaurant.

It would be rude of me to appear better informed, so I say,

let's ask Du to pick the restaurant.

While I write Du, Kubayashi goes back to the only thing that

amuses him these days—watching his cat go out and come in.

Augury

On an uncommonly warm October morning

mist shrouded mountains

dream of the Song Dynasty

crows stand in mid-air

conjuring Canada geese

who appear and disappear along ridge lines

apricot-colored leaves drift from quaking aspens

Last night an immense moon rose

through the trees like a spaceship

glazing the world silver

in the morning it was gold.

Visiting My Sister

I am visiting my sister, an old lady in Long Beach,
we live many hours apart, don't see each other often,
but we're close, for us, phone each other regularly,
share what there is to share of our narrowing lives.

When she sold her house and moved here
I teased her about joining the league of old ladies
summering on the Boardwalk, hibernating all winter,
but our phone calls didn't reveal what I see now.

I'm surprised by the old woman who opens the door,
my sister of the torpedo tits, the wet dream body
of my adolescence, has gone slack, spectral,
her clothes hang on her like a scarecrow's.

Later we head out for lunch; she's on the first floor
but there are four steps down to the sidewalk.
Years younger, I become an older brother,
holding one hand while her other holds the handrail.

I watch her hesitant steps, I whisper, *be careful!*
I'm so focused on her, I stumble on the bottom step,
saved by the firm grip of her steadying hand.
You be careful, she says.

Slide Show

After the holiday meal of too much—too much—
my sister announces; *We just got new slides back!*
We've been through this before, our just desserts.
The lights lowered, the carousel clicks and slaps,
a blurred world slowly twisted into focus,
a few clicks later pedestrians are on their heads
buildings balanced on their roofs. We love it.

My sister prompts my brother-in-law, the Saint,
to narrate but he can't remember whether
that building is in Vienna or Brussels,
whether a garden is in Holland or Brittany.
She complains, he's not a real traveler,
he actually looks forward to coming home.
She could stay away forever.

She's right; what the Saint likes is tits and
he's salted the carousel with a few full frontals.
Whenever one of his slides pops up my sister makes
an annoyed *tsk*, clicks past while we clamor—go back!
In truth, my sister's annoyance is pretense,
we all love the Saint and he's told me more than once
the reason he married my sister is her rack.

The memory is thirty years old,

the Saint's been dead the last fifteen

and my sister is in the hospital

on a trip she doesn't have to worry about

coming home from.

Say Grace

What I like about Grace is that she's easy
to be with the way girls who like guys are.
She has a combination of sweet ingenue looks
with a sparingly-used, but perfectly-timed mouth
like a trucker I find endlessly entertaining.
We'd dated years ago, married others, divorced.
When we met again, she seemed the same Grace
except for the addition of a very noticeable cross.
We went out to dinner, had fun knocking our exes;
I wondered why we'd stopped seeing each other.
I couldn't remember. Grace couldn't remember.
We'd made love back when we were seeing each other
and I was thinking, *Let's go back to my place,*
but didn't say it because it was early and that cross.
When dinner arrived, Grace asked me to say Grace,
I said, "I'm a little rusty, you say it." She did.
I went back to thinking about her coming to my place.
She had a different plan, she wanted me to come to
a Bible study class the next evening. I told her my plan.
She said, "I'm born again; I don't do that anymore,
not outside the sanctified state of holy matrimony.
Come to my Bible study, you'll love our pastor!"
"After that," I asked, "can we go to my place?"
She was getting pissed; "Listen,

no one can enter the temple of my body

now without first fucking marrying me."

I couldn't help but smile, she was irresistible.

"What?" She said.

"I was thinking of Oscar Levant's line about Doris Day,

'I knew her before she was a virgin.' "

She smiled.

I asked, "What time's the class?"

Her Name

Sometimes I come upon her name,

first thing I remember is

how she disliked it,

though disliked is putting it mildly.

This didn't matter to anyone

except her mother

who thought it a rejection,

perhaps expected from a teenager,

but odd

persisting into middle age.

She disliked it first

because it was her mother's,

boring and ordinary,

on a par with Jane Doe,

but lacking that name's mystery,

proof her parents had no imagination,

no interest or worse,

wanted her to be ordinary,

though if that was the intent,

it failed.

Of course, for years now

when I come upon her name,

it's simply a name many share,

she has no double.

I know,

I've looked.

Though that's the sort of thing she'd enjoy,

someone in a parallel universe

stuck being her,

when she didn't want to be her.

Once I asked her to a work dinner,

she said she couldn't possibly come,

not that evening,

then showed up,

confessed she'd always known she'd come,

but wanted to surprise me,

by cloning herself into the one

who couldn't be there,

and one who was,

like it was a magic trick.

→

Or the night she said,

I think of us as a threesome.

Lucky you with two women,

one in your bed,

another in your head,

she can stay as long as you want.

I said, not for the first time,

I have no idea what you're talking about.

No, she said, you don't.

That's how she told me.

Red Rover

I dreamt last night of playing Red Rover
as we did in the long twilight of summer.

Someone was calling from the other side,
Red Rover, Red Rover, Let Joanie come over!

Joan, my older sister and I, holding hands
holding hands, standing side by side,

I don't remember her playing Red Rover,
but last night she was there on our side.

And when she let my hand go and went over,
I knew she would not be coming back.

Mourning Becomes Her

Her first words to me that summer were, *I heard your father died.*

I nodded my head, expecting her to say she was sorry like everyone
  else.

I wasn't at an age when I wanted attention,

my father's death embarrassed me. I didn't want to talk about it.

But she didn't say that, she asked what he died of (cancer),

then when (a week ago), and did I see him die (no!).

She said she would have liked to come to the wake.

I told her Jews don't have wakes, she said she knew that.

I really like wakes, we Irish have great wakes

but I haven't been to one in months.

Mary and I had barely spoken before; I knew her brother who was
  my age

but she was a year older than us at an age when a year made a dif-
  ference.

My Mum and I talk about who died all the time, she reads the obits

first thing when the paper comes.

A few days later she asked if I'd like to go to a funeral.

"With your mother?" I asked.

No, the family is going visiting today, I don't want to.

It's at St. Ignatius, I don't know who died, it doesn't matter.

I knew the church; I'd been there to wait for my friend Matt when he had to go to confession. I liked going there.

We sat in the back, she told me I didn't have to do anything.

She went to light a candle while I waited in the pew.

Those days the mass was in Latin and everyone but me

knew what to say, when to sit, stand, or kneel.

I watched Mary, kept quiet, did what she did.

We stayed till the coffin was wheeled down the aisle

and most of the people had left the church,

then she took my hand and led me to a small side room.

The walls were lined with pictures of Saints

with rows of candles in front of them.

No one was there.

As the Saints looked on, she kissed me, kissed me hard.

Black Olives

Even if, characterologically speaking,

you're an asshole,

your mind does not process memories

the way your body processes pizza.

So, the pizza with black olives you ate

thirty years ago will not be seen again.

Yet the memory of that uncharacteristically happy day,

who you shared the pizza with

the thrill of behaving badly

her head hovering over yours eclipsing the sun

giving her an ironic halo

prompting thoughts, at that incongruous moment,

of Russian Orthodox iconography

her heavy cross swinging like Foucault's pendulum

threatening to crack your tooth,

still visits you unmoored from time,

now as much fantasy as memory

continually revised by yourself, *the script doctor*,

in endless rehearsals administering CPR

hoping for a repeat performance

before the final curtain.

Slickrock

On a solitary morning walk along the slickrock,
I recall why this sandpapery sandstone terrain
carries this odd, old cowboy name.
American Indians rode their horses on rimrock
bare-hooved, sure-footed,
but clad with iron shoes, the cowboy's horses
tended to lose their footing.
Sudden drop-offs into deep crevices
and canyons made it a troubling place
for a horse to lose its footing.

The sudden clattering of hooves losing their grip,
the cowboy's yelp and *whoa*
the slap of horseflesh hitting the slickrock,
then, in slow motion, the terrified white-eyed
horse struggling to regain its footing,
the bewildered, open-mouthed rider,
cinched together, sliding over the edge
into history and language.

The Girls

That's what you called them
the summer we found each other,
the summer I tried to persuade you,
If you close your eyes, I can't see you.
You said you weren't that stupid,
but you closed your eyes a lot that summer.
Not that much happened, it was the 50's,
not like now; we were both surprised
by what we did, never talked about it.
I was too shy to talk about anything,
I was surprised I was doing anything,
these feelings, these changes in my body,
this hunger to touch a girl where you
weren't supposed to, were new to me.
I'm not sure how the touching started
I think it started with kissing,
practicing kissing like in the movies,
and soon kissing so hard my lips swelled,
maybe yours did too but I never knew.
You'd kiss with your eyes closed
your teeth clenched against my tongue.
I touched your breasts lightly after a while
surprised you didn't say no.
You called them, the girls, and when I asked,

Can the girls come out to play?

You said, *No.* And they never did.

But you allowed me to touch them

to feel your nipples grow hard as I did.

Kitsilano

Women in black burkinis gather on the sandy beach,
watch their children learn how to clam at the water's edge
from other children whose only common tongue is childhood.

Nearby lithe young women sunbathe topless, chatting,
listening to music. Teenage boys tossing a Frisbee
edge closer, working hard pretending not to notice.

Young mothers breastfeed infants discreetly under cover,
while older ones casually lift a breast out of their swimsuits,
brush off sand, and nurse eager toddlers nestled in their laps.

A young Sikh couple on their honeymoon takes selfies with an old
35 mm camera on a tripod. He, in turban and sports jacket, sets up
the time delay shot, then hurries to the side of his modest wife,
taking shot after shot, blushing and laughing;
their joy embarrasses them.

An aged Asian couple, defeated by rented beach chairs,
is rescued by two dashiki-clad men from Ghana twice their size.

In late afternoon mothers and grandmothers
yell at their children to come out of the water
in English, Hindi, Farsi, Korean, and Tagalog.

The children resist in every language
and plunge deeper into the sea.

Rattled

We're hiking at Arches National Park in southern Utah.

My son has hiked there before, this was my first.

The warnings posted along the trail,

and my overactive imagination, did not help.

I stepped carefully, listened and watched

for the telltale coil and rattle,

until the steady climb and mid-day heat

pushed my caution aside.

We stopped to take a drink,

but when my son turned to go on, he heard a rattle.

Don't move, he whispered, and looked around,

but could see nothing, the only place he couldn't

see was in the deep shade of a sage bush behind me.

When the rattle reached my ear, I slowly stepped away.

Still we could see nothing, but the rattle quieted

and with no coil in sight we continued on our way.

Happy for the small excitement, and a story to tell.

New Year's Day

It's morning on a chilly New Year's Day
and only you and the children are not hungover.
The TV is on as always and the entire family is here,
even more oblivious than usual, mutely watching
the Rose Bowl Parade from sunny Pasadena.

When the float from the Shriners Hospital for Children,
escorted by fez-topped clowns on tiny tricycles,
comes on the screen, your eyes fill.
An announcer says it's made of forty-thousand red and white
chrysanthemums, and thirty-thousand blue forget-me-nots.

The forget-me-nots start your slow trickle of tears,
ignored by all but the smallest child in the room, who,
like a nurse out of options in the middle of a long night,
comes to you and holds your hand,
a home remedy older than words.

At the Cancer Clinic

(for Norm Nichols)

He was waiting for his chemo,
she, an infusion of platelets.
They'd seen each other there before,
and when he waved,
she came to sit with him.
They didn't know how much time they'd have;
she felt an urgency to tell him who she was.

I was a hidden child in Poland,
do you know what that means?
I was six or seven when the war ended,
the only survivor in my family.
The people who hid me didn't want me,
I was too nervous, too needy,
the Joint took me to Israel with other orphans,
we grew up on a kibbutz.

When I was old enough, I went to Spain,
Barcelona, to be a flamenco dancer.
I thought of myself as a Gypsy;
I don't know why; they were hated too.
Sometimes you just want to be somebody else.

I married three times: the first, the best,
died young, the second I left, the third left me.

After Barcelona, I went back to Israel,
toured with a flamenco troupe,
we went to the United States,
Argentina, Spain then Israel again.

I moved to Big Sur with my third husband,
that was some place!

Now I'm here with my daughter,
though I'm not always sure where here is.

I have three children—

his name was being called—

please wait for me after,

I haven't even begun to tell you.

Shoah

A daughter of holocaust survivors,
immersed in the survivor community,
an academic studying the impact of trauma
and its mystifying transmission
into the next generation.

She was driven, smart, funny, sarcastic, an intensity
that shrouded a vast sadness, a hidden tenderness.

Everyone who confronts the holocaust is shaken;
up close it's unbearable, the pain of victims,
the ordinariness of the perpetrators, the evil.
We worked to bring the stories of the Holocaust
and its survivors to a wider audience —

Survivors who found the courage to speak
for the many who lived like ghosts in the shadows.

We flirted a little, argued a little, liked each other,
got things done; though never enough, never enough.
At one event, we listened to Elie Wiesel speak fervently,
eloquently as the audience applauded over and over.
She whispered, *There's no business like Shoah business.*

We live among ashes, the faint odor of smoke
reminding us of who we are, what world we live in.

Another Kind of Jewish Family

In our New York Jewish intellectual family it was hard to get a word in at the table. (Erica Jong)

We ate in silence like chrysalises in cocoons

doing our time waiting for our wings to unfurl

hoping not to be noticed by the god of thunder

doing our best to make our presence an absence

our heads down watching the vipers coil

around our milk glasses watching every move.

We were dry tinder focused on the swirling clouds

of sadness and loss that no one ever spoke of

we knew how the air could change,

that feeling of static electricity building

we sat waiting for the lightning to strike,

no one wanted to be there

everyone was innocent

everyone was guilty,

spoons misplaced among the knives.

One Autumn in New York

There is infinite hope in the universe, but not for us. (Franz Kafka)

I am walking across Sixth Avenue
from the parking garage to my office.
It's a glorious day with a rare New York City blue sky.
Downtown, in the distance, the sun glints off the Twin Towers.
The clear, crisp air put a spring in everyone's step,
heralding the start of another perfect autumn in New York.

In two hours, every siren in the city will be wailing.

Anticipation

Hurricanes, forecast days in advance,
like end of term papers assigned the first day,
tend to be ignored until the last moment
when threats from officials like untenured teachers,
reach a fearsome pitch imploring us to prepare,
fill gas tanks, buy water, D cells, non-perishables.
Yet early forecasts make a storm seem such
a slow locomotive we laze on the track
until the first bands of rain and gusting winds.

Then when all is ready,
apartment cleaned, pantry stocked, shower taken;
the long-anticipated guest veers off,
and we're left abandoned, feeling foolish
sitting in imagined darkness,
flicking the flashlight on and off,
eating our emergency M & M's.

Flying in Winter

A hurried trip for an unhappy reason left us
grounded in a snow storm at O'Hare.
To get to know an airport, you need to be stranded
with delays becoming cancellations,
today becoming tomorrow.
Then you can appreciate its architecture,
the latest factory black duct work hung
from steel girders, banks of fluorescents
dropping gloom
on Crayola-colored plastic seats
designed to thwart vandals and sleep.
It's late, most concessions are dark,
those open have little food, their tired workers
want to go home to their children.

And here we sit, clutching compassion-rate tickets,
drifting in and out of sleep, wondering if
it is we who are dead, and O'Hare, hell.

Her Collection

My elderly Aunt has selected her favorite photographs
from family albums passed down over the years,
placed them in old frames bought at the Five & Dime
downtown when there was a Five & Dime downtown.
She re-reads letters written to her mother by Uncle Joe
when he was overseas during the war, she'd forgotten
she had them, and decides to set them on the end table
as though they'd arrived in this morning's mail.
Last month she found a White Owl cigar box in the attic
that had a cat's eye aggie and a pure white shooter,
(she's surprised at the names she remembers and forgets)
there was a 1906 Indian head, a 1943 steel penny
and a copper one from the year she was born.
She placed them in an ashtray with a perfect shell
from a forgotten childhood beach.

She likes these things close, it reminds her,
I had a life too, a thought that steadies her
the way a tightrope walker is steadied
by a balance pole as they teeter
above the abyss.

One Morning

Inevitably you'll wake one morning
only to discover that you didn't
and once you stop waking up
it's a hard habit to break
and after the surprise, it's not bad.
Your memory, that had been slowly
slipping away for years, is gone.
You can't even remember being alive,
so, there's no sense of loss.

Actually, it's sort of Zen,
not in the sense of struggling
to achieve **no mind**, just noticing
you have no mind, without noticing
anything has been lost or achieved.
And it's perfect just the way it is.
So perfect you don't even notice it,
you're just that Zen.

What Remains

Genes shared with others in ever diminishing fractions,
reflecting a decreasing investment in a future
that no longer includes you.

Your clothes given to the Salvation Army,
one day a man who once worked with you at GE
will look up in a mall and say, *I know that shirt.*

A few beats later, he'll remember you,
remember you're dead, but he'll think of you
and GE's shuttered factory the rest of the day.

You never gave much thought to life as you lived it
but you helped people who came to you needing it,
listened when someone needed someone to listen.

There was a time you helped a driver with a flat tire
that changed, not the driver's life, but the life of a shy
seven-year-old in the car you smiled and winked at.

A soldier who survived the war you never talked about;
he was the enemy; he wouldn't have known what hit him,
but by then you just wanted to go home and you both did.

Remember the baseball, the one you waited hours
outside the Polo Grounds for Willie Mays to sign?
A foul ball he hit that you caught.

Your great grandchild found it in a junk drawer,
took it to a park for a pick-up game with his best friend,
a friend who looks a lot like the "Say Hey Kid."

The "Kid" hit it over the right field fence for a home run,
the ball landed in the tall grass and was never found.
It's still there, the autograph faded, invisible.

I Listened to a TED Talk on Dying So You Don't Have To

The best thing about dying is not being there,

like you weren't there when you were born.

You don't remember being born, your mother

remembers it, but you don't, not like you

remember your first car or broken bone.

As death nears, the body, the mind

has its anesthesia, it always did and now

there are meds and, believe me,

everyone wants you to miss the end.

You'll never forget the moment you got

the final diagnosis, where you were,

the face of who told you, the words they used,

your flood of disbelief, then anger,

even sympathy for the person telling you,

but death is different, there's nothing to fear,

you won't even be there.

In fact, as it draws close, it will feel

like you were never actually here at all.

That's a good thing, because if you were alert

and present, you might realize this is

your last chance to tell your wife you

always hated the way she breathes,

and you blame your cancer on her meatloaf

and you want a do-over because

this trip sucked and you deserve a chance

to do a life without meatloaf,

maybe as a pirate, or a long-distance trucker,

but you'll be zonked on meds

so, all the assembled will recall is that you muttered

something about meatloaf or pirates which

they'll think was about the musician or the meds.

So, forget deathbed monologues,

they'll only piss your heirs off

and they'll bury you in a cardboard coffin.

There's something else you should know,

people will visit at the end, dead people.

It's another good thing about dying,

it feels like a family reunion, a party

with people who've been gone for years,

dogs show up and while you're busy talking,

you'll cross over and be dead and you'll be

so pleased to see your mother or, at least

your old dog, you won't even notice.

Old Jack

After Old Jack had shown me how to trap the raccoons

that were killing our chickens—with #2 legholds

and canned sardines—I went by his place to tell him

I'd gotten six setting the traps, like he said, at first dark,

then going out at first light to shoot them with a .22.

"What did you do with them raccoons?"

I told him I'd buried them.

"I wish you hadn't done that, my grandson Hanley

could've skinned them, he needs the practice."

I told him, "If I get more, I'll remember Hanley."

A friend of Old Jack came walking out of the woods

behind his place but hesitated when he saw me.

Jack noticed; told him he should come sit down

nodded toward me, "He's okay," introduced us,

and with a wink at me, added, "He's a trapper!"

Euey seemed duly impressed and it fell to me

to explain what I'd trapped, how Jack had helped.

We sat looking at each other a moment,

I said, "I needed to do something about the chickens,

but to be honest, I hated everything about it."

I felt like hell every time I had to shoot a raccoon.

I expected them to smile at my tender feelings,

but they nodded and Euey started talking about

his putting old Molly down a few days ago

when she got so poorly, she could barely walk.
We sat there a moment in silence and Jack said,
"Molly was a damn smart dog, if she got on a scent,
whatever she was tracking was getting treed.
She was a genuine Plott hound,
there's not many of them around here."
Talk of Molly got Jack and Euey talking about dogs,
hunting with them, remembering old favorites,
gone now. Tears leaked from wet eyes,
got brushed away like flies, without comment.
These were hard men who never had much.
They wouldn't pay a vet to put a dog down, but it
wasn't the money, it was a matter of whose dog it was.
It was your dog, so it was your job. It's that simple.
You get attached to dogs, they're part of the family,
sometimes the best part.

No one likes to kill anything,
but there comes a time when it needs doing,
and you do it.

Sweet

"Sweet for sweet," he said,
as we swapped our honey
for his maple syrup
in a town where earlier ways lingered,
our eggs, blueberries swapped
at Sykes General Store
for whatever we needed,
home baked muffins, nails, washers.
The tomatoes and beets we had
for sweet corn we always wanted.

Cash poor people, rich in older ways,
a sense of place, knowing the land,
knowing the stories, knowing each other
for generations,
father and son,
mother and daughter,
neighbors who welcomed us
people we could count on
when help was needed
people we wanted to count on us,
Sweet for sweet.

Pandemic

Now that Covid-19 has clarified matters,
I'm feeling somewhat encouraged that we're all,
in a manner of speaking, on the same page and
can agree, that from the moment of conception,
Mother Nature, as if in the grip of creator's remorse,
is doing her best to kill us, the more of us there are,
the harder she tries. Eight billion people using
her as a dump and sewer was not her plan.

Forgiving our trespasses has its limits.
When Mother Nature creates new diseases
and perpetuates old ones, who can blame her?
But retail deaths, one here, one there, take forever.

So, periodically she goes wholesale; wars help,
but to make the big quotas sing you need pandemics
like the Black Plague, Spanish flu, Covid-19 or
some other teeming petri dish of lurking nasties
waiting to devour your organs the way Uncle Irv
works his way through the buffet at family weddings.

Mother Nature wants a little peace and quiet.
She has a plan.
We may not like it.

Buoyancy

As soon as you learn they're at Jones Beach
the surf high, the undertow strong,
the child small, the mother preoccupied;
you become a witness anxiously watching.

He won't drown, the problem is he misses her,
she's changed, he can't grasp exactly how,
she doesn't smile, doesn't talk, it frightens him.
He stands in the surf, looks at her vacant face.

He's taught himself the *Dead Man's float*
he wants her to think he's drowning
wants her to cry out, to run to him.
But she's looked away, lit a cigarette.

She doesn't notice his laughable behind
bobbing in the surf, defeating him, revealing him;
a red-faced Stanislavski rehearsing
his desperation before an empty theater.

Decades later walking past a phone booth
he will see a woman on a call crying,
their eyes meet, she angrily turns away.
He will dream of her for months.

Chasing Rabbits

We were day-glow color wheels

ecstatic synesthetes

shooting blue sparks from snapping fingers

cartwheeling through the doors of perception

opened by orange sunshine dots

catapulting through day after day lighter than air

living on brownies, Rocky Road, the Grateful Dead...

when we felt the tug of gravity's leash

a scratch in the vinyl that held us static.

It was over

our certainty fled

our legs leadened,

the colors drained

exhausted

we were cast into stillness

the stillness of the rabbit

crouching in the tall grass

as the fox stops—

sniffs the air—

tenses.

Ticket to Ride

Anyone with a sense of plot or narrative line
asks when did it begin, what was going on,
thinking it's a diagrammable phenomenon
that Sherlock Holmes could logically deduce
or Dr. Laszlo Kreizler might investigate and diagnose.
But it's not like that, it's more like walking,
I crawled then I walked, not to escape from crawling,
I found I could, and did, but no one inquired
why had you begun walking that particular day?
What was going on, eh?
Moving into a book is like that, first I learned to read,
then this new possibility arose, I went from there.
No trauma, I wasn't unhappy; my life was like most.
I found I had the gift of entering a story,
not as a named character, someone that moved the plot,
but a gift for fitting in, blending, like an extra in a film.
It would be weird if the main characters
were the only people in the restaurant scene
or the only ones on a bus. It came easy to me.
On one page I might be a passenger on the Paris train,
the next a passerby on the Rue des Rêves;
we're needed to create the world of the book.
I wonder sometimes why everyone doesn't do it,
but you have to have the gift of finding the door,

the right frame of mind to slip out of this world
into a novel one.

There are others like me, each with preferences,
I stay away from science fiction or horror;
what appeals to me is adventure, mysteries, spies.
It's an immense world compared to this one, in fact
I'm going back soon, there's a new book coming out,
a magical writer, it starts in a Grand Railway station,
its brass doors are beckoning me as we speak,
I'll be in the ticket line, then a passenger on the train,
I know this writer; it'll be an adventure, late 1890's
travel to the far reaches of Asia, spies, plot twists.
Some people think it must get boring over time
but it's not like that, whenever a new reader
picks up the book we're all on page one,
none of us knows what happens next
until the reader turns the page.

Deer Hunting

1.

We moved to the country,
to property neighbors said
was a good place to hunt deer.
I gave my neighbors permission to hunt,
to be neighborly,
but I didn't hunt.

I had nothing against hunting,
but I didn't hunt.
I saw deer regularly those days,
does, fawns, spike horns,
but deer with big racks were rare
until I learned where the big bucks hid.

If anyone asked if I'd seen any,
I'd send them off in the wrong direction,
then after listening to my misinformation
a neighbor shot an eight-point buck.
Local deer-hunting news spreads fast,
lying had given me credibility.

I got invitations to hunt
I resisted, until I didn't.
I got a license, a slug gun
blasted away.
I learned how close I'd need to be
to kill a deer. Very close.

I usually hunted with a neighbor my age
who was mostly over hunting
so, our hunt
was a stroll in the woods,
long sessions of quiet watching,
our backs propped against old sugar maples.

Sometimes we saw deer,
but too far away to shoot.
My buddy would say,
Thank God that deer didn't get closer,
what the hell would we do with a dead deer,
we'd have a heart attack dragging it out.

$\longrightarrow$

2.

On a Saturday morning,
in late November I awoke to find
it snowing lightly,
a few inches already down,
easy tracking weather
a perfect day for an early hunt.

I walked alone to the upper meadow,
settled myself in the stand of trees
that lined the meadow and waited.
By now it was snowing heavily,
I could barely see the thirty yards
which was as far as I would shoot.

Then I saw something,
but wasn't sure what,
I looked through the gun's scope
thought I saw a large coyote,
then realized it was a buck walking
up a rise straight toward me.

I saw the snow on his back, his head,
even lining each tine
of his large rack,
more dream than deer.

As he drew closer,
I knew I could kill him.

I thought about it
a long moment
pointed the sight at his heart
then slid on the safety
and walked out toward the buck
waving my arms.

Get out of here,
go bed down,
you're gonna get shot!
The buck stopped,
strained to see me through
the heavy snow,

then wheeled around
in slow motion,
and pranced back down
across the meadow.
The rising wind and swirling
snow sent me home.

$\rightarrow$

I told the story to my buddy,
soon everyone heard it.
Said it was buck fever, but it wasn't,
it was my imagination,
if I pulled the trigger,
I could see the buck falling,

could see its blood splattering
the white field,
could see its legs
churning the soft snow.
I could see it.
I didn't want it.

Our meeting was perfect
the way it was.
The image of the buck
walking to me with snow on its back
must have been what I was hunting for
all along, I was done hunting.

I talked about it endlessly,
non-hunting friends congratulated me
for not shooting,
but the hunters were even
more touched and pleased.

Nobody loves deer more than deer hunters.

3.

A month later on the winter solstice
I was staring out the window into
our yard lit by light from the house,
it was snowing again and I saw
a doe walk into the yard,
then another until there were six

then the big buck walked in.
This was his herd
and their visit on this
most auspicious night
felt ineffably connected
to our earlier meeting.

We looked at each other
for a long time
then one after another,
without a backward glance,
they walked out of the light
into the dark woods.

Shadow

You know how at the end of the day I like to walk the path

that marks the borders of our small farm and woodlot.

You call it, *patrolling my known world.*

But this evening it was different; odd, unsettling.

I hope if I tell you, the strangeness will diminish

the way shame or fear is lessened when it's shared.

You know how I am; I would protect us from harm,

not bring it home. But tonight, I felt I was followed,

regret coming directly home, though the home lights

looked so like a safe harbor through the deep woods,

I couldn't help myself. I should have thought of it before,

but I was unnerved, as if I'd seen a ghost,

knowing full well there are no ghosts.

Maybe I was overtired, or it was a trick of the eye, or shadows.

What I'm saying is, whatever it seemed; it's not.

I was walking the path that runs along the stone wall

when some movement caught my eye, a bird or squirrel.

It was slipping beyond the hour of deep shadow into dusk,

yet it seemed to me light enough to see.

I looked toward the movement, saw nothing but a shadow,

though I thought for an instant of a drawing of a family,

like you might see in a child's picture book.

When I looked again, I thought I saw a woman,

someone who looked familiar, someone I've seen before,

but long ago, walking with a little girl.

As I walked on, they walked along with me

on the other side of the wall moving neither closer, nor away.

Nothing was said. I heard only my footsteps on the fallen leaves,

yet as I turned toward home, I felt I was followed.

It was a feeling, I didn't look.

Look at what, I said to myself, *there's nothing there!*

Where they are now, I don't know.

I don't know what to think; if I look,

they might be standing at the door

or maybe they're back on the other side.

Though as I say this, I wonder if

as we get close to leaving this world,

we get a glimpse of the world to come,

see others who've crossed over

as you have and I will soon enough.

That would be a gift,

a hint that when we get there, we won't be so alone,

a barely noticeable sign, the way in winter there comes a day

that says Spring is on its way.

Maybe what I saw was like that,

a glimpse there's something beyond the wall

we were once so certain marked the end.

On the Royal Road

My eyes open, I blink, look around and realize,
I'm here, it's the road from Frampol to Zamosc.

How I got here is a mystery, how I know where I am,
yet another.

I remember I was reading "Gimpel the Fool,"
I must have fallen asleep, I'm dreaming.

I close my eyes expecting
to wake in my own living room.
Instead, I wake in the same spot;
this is no dream.

I walk toward Zamosc, yet arrive in Frampol,
a large town built around a market square,
I walk around, but I know no one
so like a character in a Singer story,
I go to the synagogue to ask the Rabbi's help.
The Rabbi assumes I've come to Frampol
because of some family connection,
when I tell him my name, he seems to recall it,
though in a tentative way I take as a kindness.
The Rabbi seems concerned, even worried,

he doesn't know what to make of me, I can't blame him.

I can't explain where I'm from or how I got there.
I was reading in 2020, but here it's years earlier,
there are no cars, only horses and wagons,
no telephones or electric wires or lights.

How can I say I came from a book, another time?
Whatever his concerns, he says, I'm welcome
to sleep at the synagogue and eat with his family.

When I ask about leaving Frampol that's another story,
I could walk, but there are problems in all directions;
the only safe exit for a Jew in Frampol is the grave.

That's not the only problem; after a few minutes I realize
the Rabbi must speak Yiddish and I speak English,
how are we talking? When I ask the Rabbi, he's confused.

I say, *I speak English*, but the Rabbi says he hears Yiddish;
I say, *You speak English*, he insists he's speaking Yiddish.

Now he's looking at me with greater concern.

$\rightarrow$

He's thinking hard about getting me out of Frampol
and recalls a shopkeeper who goes to Zamosc weekly.
He'll arrange for me to go with him.

With this I join him for afternoon and evening prayers,
then dinner with his family and a few aged congregants.

That night I try to sleep, but I'm troubled by the thought
these people will be murdered by the Nazi's in 1939. I lie awake
worrying about how to warn the Rabbi;
I'm certain he won't believe me; he'll think I'm a lunatic.
I could come to no solution, but as dawn was breaking
I finally fall asleep and awake at home.

Ruth asks if I'd had a good nap.
Why am I here? I ask.
"Where should you be?"
I try to explain what happened,
I insist I need to return, to warn the Rabbi.
"You were dreaming."
It wasn't a dream!
I describe Frampol, the shul, the Rabbi, his family;
yet with each passing moment, the images fade,
my memories dissolve, until there's nothing.
I desperately wanted to return.
Ruth grew impatient and annoyed,

"What you hope to do can't be done, you can't change the past."

When I was there what has passed was still in the future,

Ruth, I must warn them!

"No, you must accept what happened has happened."

I had a chance.

"You had a dream."

The Birthday Party

It was at Matt McKay's birthday party that
I realized not everyone got underwear for their birthday;
some kids got things they wanted.
Not that I always got underwear, sometimes I got socks.
But his mother gave him a "Gene Autry 44" cap gun
with a "Genuine Leather Quick Draw Holster."
Matt's family was rich; me and Joey,
the other neighbor boy Matt invited, weren't,
neither of us had even had a birthday party.
(This wasn't even his real birthday party,
that was on Saturday and didn't include Joey or me;
he got a "Red Ryder" BB gun at that party!)

This was the summer when cap pistols were all we wanted,
that, and rolls and rolls of caps, which were cheap,
so even I had caps long before I had a cap pistol.
Cheap cap guns cost two dollars, and a gun as nice as Matt's
cost way more, a holster was beyond my dreams.
I pulled weeds, cut lawns, collected deposit bottles
along the railroad tracks for weeks to get enough for a cap pistol.
Until then I'd pop the caps with a rock.
Saving was hard; no penny candy or ice pops for weeks.
I wish I could say it was worth it, but the anticipation,
the longing, the saving for the cap pistol was the best part.

After a week of shooting my cap pistol

from morning till night, I was over it.

Though, sitting with Matt and Joey that day,

eating birthday cake and trying to remember

to say *please* and *thank you* to Mrs. McKay—

who looked like a movie star—

that was still a lesson I wouldn't grasp for decades.

Whiskey Down!

Two over easy, bacon side, whiskey down!

That was my introduction to diner slang,
dad and I off somewhere early in the morning,
probably a pigeon show,
somewhere my sister or mother wouldn't want to go.
This was my first time in a diner and I was just
tall enough to slide my behind up on the counter stool.
Behind is what we called it at home,
but I knew older boys called it a *butt*,
though I didn't know then that butt had two t's
and the but I knew had only one.
I knew there were cigarette butts
and the neighbor's goat Skippy would butt you,
and I bet there were other buts,
but I didn't know any more.
I watched the waitress move like a juggler,
balancing plates and coffee cups,
her cigarette bouncing between dark red lips,
pacing along the counter bringing full plates,
one-way empties on the way back,
the cook in the kitchen putting a new plate
up on the order shelf as she takes one off.

I figured out about the eggs and bacon,

that's what my father ordered,

but he was drinking coffee, not whiskey.

After I got my pancakes, the place quieted down,

and the waitress came over to my dad.

They talked like they knew each other;

no one talked to me.

She had very long black hair, and I wondered

what someone with that color hair was called.

I'd heard of blonds, redheads, even brunettes

because my older sister said she was one,

even though she had brown hair like me.

Maybe the waitress was a blackhead;

I knew something else was a blackhead,

but I wasn't sure what.

An Eclipse in Stephentown

May 10, 1994. Start, 10:49 AM. Totality, 12:36 PM. End 2:20 PM.

Night was falling in the midst of morning.
The chickens, as confused as I was
by the changing light, the unnatural hush,
ran into their coops as if the eerie darkening
were a predatory shadow descending from on high.

I felt the same, even knowing what to expect
did not diminish my sense of impending apocalypse.

Call it the trauma of bewilderment,
call it the dread of wonder,
call it the beginning of prayer—
or the need for it.

The Boy Who Loved Pigeons

The boy who loved pigeons was sad,
for he grew as a boy does,
without the feathers he hoped for,
or the wings that could lift him
out of his pedestrian life.

He imagined flying with his pigeons,
felt certain his pigeons were surprised he didn't,
for he was one of their flock
as surely as they were his family.

Pigeons were gentle and devoted to their young,
keeping them warm, patiently feeding them,
sitting with them day and night. It was the way
he wanted to be if he had children.

Once, when his pigeons were out flying,
two disappeared, a young one and its mother.
He thought maybe they had flown too far, got lost.
Day after day, first thing in the morning
last thing before dark, he would look for them.
Finally, he grew certain they were killed by hawks.
Then three weeks later, there they were on the loft.
He opened their door, they went in, ate, and drank.   →

He held the mother, she seemed thin but okay,
but when he picked the young one up,
he saw a big gash under one wing,
crusted over, and almost healed.

He knew then what happened.
A hawk attacked it while it was flying
with the flock miles from home;
it had struggled and broken free,
but was too injured to fly home.
Its mother had stayed with it, cared for it,
until it healed enough to fly.

He was sure it was exactly what happened,
even if some people might not believe him.
Pigeons loved their young, loved their home,
as the boy hoped someday to love his home.
It didn't matter their home was small,
made from wood the boy took from lots
where new houses were being built.

Once a hurricane broke branches off trees
and blew their little loft on to its side
so that its door was on the top.
The boy worried the pigeons were hurt,
feared they'd be afraid of their home,

but when he climbed up and lifted the door,
they flew out and walked around their loft,
looking again and again at the strange scene,
first with one eye then the other.

He fretted they wouldn't come back
after he righted and repaired the loft,
but as it grew late, they flew to the loft.
Because when you love your home,
all that matters is that it's your home.

In time the boy grew up and married,
had children, tried to treat them and his wife
the way a pigeon would, even if it wasn't easy.
He lived a long life, and wherever he lived,
he always kept his pigeons.

When he was very old,
his wife died, his children moved,
they had families of their own.
He was alone again with his pigeons.
He felt content to sit in the loft,
visiting his pigeons, letting them out to fly
on each nice day, morning and afternoon.

$\longrightarrow$

One day, while sitting in the yard watching them fly,
he felt a bad pain in his chest; it took his breathe away.
He was very still, and when he looked into the sky,
he noticed his small pigeon flock seemed larger.

He saw pigeons flying in from every point of the compass
until he couldn't count them all. It wasn't unusual for his flock to
pick up a stray, usually a tired and lost racing homer,
but he'd never seen this many pigeons.

He whistled to call his flock down;
slowly they dropped out of the larger flock.
He expected the others would fly away,
but they followed his birds down,
and as they landed on the roof or the grass,
he could see some of them looked familiar.

Then an old favorite hen of his,
one he hadn't seen since he was a boy,
landed at his feet, flew up to his shoulder
to sit as she had years ago.

How was this possible?

The old man was overjoyed, but confused.
Where had these birds been all these years?

How could it be the same ones,

even ones he knew for certain were dead?

One after another he recognized his old birds,

they had all come back to him.

He had to tell his children,

the guys at the pigeon club and feed store.

The hen ran her beak through his hair,

flew down to the ground and then—

as if by an invisible sign—

they gathered at his feet and looked skyward.

He knew they were preparing to take off.

As he watched, a few did take off.

He called, *wait…wait!*

He felt himself lifting from his chair.

He was flying.

He was flying.

About the Poet

Howard J. Kogan is a retired psychotherapist now living in Ashland, Massachusetts with his wife, Libby. His years of retirement have provided him with the opportunity to return to narrative poetry. His poems have appeared in *Still Crazy*, *Occu-poetry*, *Poetry Ark*, *Naugatuck River Review*, *Jewish Currents Anthology*, *Literary Gazette*, *Pathways*, *Up the River*, *Point Mass Anthology*, *Misfit Magazine*, *Flair*, *The American Jewish World*, and *Award Winning Poems from Smith's Tavern Poet Laureate Contest* (2010 and 2011 Editions). His other books of poems, *Indian Summer* and *A Chill in the Air*, are available from Square Circle Press. His chapbook, *General Store Poems*, published by Benevolent Bird Press in 2014, is available from the author.

About his writing he says, "After setting aside writing poetry in my twenties to attend to family and career, I returned to it in my sixties. I'm grateful to have this opportunity to return to an early love and give voice to the inner thoughts, perceptions, and memories that have been my constant and (mostly) welcome companions." *(Selfie courtesy of the author.)*

Indian Summer
poems by Howard J. Kogan

Howard J. Kogan began writing poetry in his twenties, but set it aside to pursue family life and a career as a social worker and psychotherapist. In his sixties he returned to writing poetry, a time he wistfully refers to as his "Indian summer." In 2011, Howard was named Poet Laureate of Smith's Tavern, an annual contest held in Voorheesville featuring the top poets of New York's Capital Region. This first collection of fifty poems includes the six he submitted for the 2010 and 2011 Smith's Tavern contests.

ISBN: 978-0-9833897-3-6
124 pages, softcover

www.SquareCirclePress.com

www.ingramcontent.com/pod-product-compliance
Lightning Source LLC
Chambersburg PA
CBHW021510090426
42739CB00007B/548